D1511395

When Daddy Hit Mommy

KIDS HAVE *TROUBLES* TOO

When Daddy Hit Mommy

by Sheila Stewart and Rae Simons

Mason Crest Publishers

MASON CREST PUBLISHERS INC.
370 Reed Road
Broomall, Pennsylvania 19008
(866)MCP-BOOK (toll free)
www.masoncrest.com

First Printing
9 8 7 6 5 4 3 2 1

CIP data on file with the Library of Congress

ISBN (set) 978-1-4222-1691-0   ISBN 978-1-4222-1696-5
ISBN (ppbk set) 978-1-4222-1904-1   ISBN 978-1-4222-1909-6 (pbk.)

Design by MK Bassett-Harvey.
Produced by Harding House Publishing Service, Inc.
www.hardinghousepages.com
Cover design by Torque Advertising + Design.
Printed in USA by Bang Prtinting.

The creators of this book have made every effort to provide accurate information, but it should not be used as a substitute for the help and services of trained professionals.

Introduction

Each child is unique—and each child encounters a unique set of circumstances in life. Some of these circumstances are more challenging than others, and how a child copes with those challenges will depend in large part on the other resources in her life.

The issues children encounter cover a wide range. Some of these are common to almost all children, including threats to self-esteem, anger management, and learning to identify emotions. Others are more unique to individual families, but problems such as parental unemployment, a death in the family, or divorce and remarriage are common but traumatic events in many children's lives. Still others—like domestic abuse, alcoholism, and the incarceration of a family member—are unfortunately not uncommon in today's world.

Whatever problems a child encounters in life, understanding that he is not alone is a key component to helping him cope. These books, both their fiction and nonfiction elements, allow children to see that other children are in the same situations. The books make excellent tools for triggering conversation in a nonthreatening way. They will also promote understanding and compassion in children who may not be experiencing these issues themselves.

These books offer children important factual information—but perhaps more important, they offer hope.

—*Cindy Croft, M.A., Ed., Director of the Center for Inclusive Child Care*

At suppertime, Daddy hadn't come home from work yet. Rose tried not to be worried, because sometimes he was late for good reasons. Sometimes his boss asked him to stay a little later. And once his car had had a flat tire on the way home. Of course, he hadn't been very happy when he did get home that time.

Mommy was nervous, too. Rose could tell because her hands were shaking, and she wasn't saying very much. When she handed Rose a stack of plates to put on the table, they almost slipped out of her hands. The only person who wasn't nervous was Rose's baby brother Brody. He was crawling around under the kitchen table, saying, "Ba ba ba ba," and eating the pieces of cracker he had dropped down there earlier.

Rose set the table, and Mommy took the chicken and rice out of the oven, but Daddy still hadn't come.

"I guess you and Brody can eat now," Mommy said finally. She was biting her thumbnail and frowning at the table. "I'll wait and eat with your Daddy."

Rose didn't think that was a good idea. Daddy didn't like anybody to eat without him.

"I'll wait too," she said. "I'm not hungry yet anyway." And that was true, because she was too nervous to be hungry. "I can feed Brody, though." She thought it was probably okay for Brody to eat, since he ate baby food.

"Okay," said Mommy. She went into the living room to look out the front window again.

Rose picked up Brody to put him in his high-chair. He was heavier than he used to be, and he was wiggly, so it was getting hard to carry him. She lugged him over to his chair and stood on her tiptoes to set him on the seat. He grabbed her hair with his sticky fingers and laughed. Rose was glad somebody could be happy.

Daddy still hadn't come home by the time Brody finished eating. Mommy was walking back and forth, from the kitchen to the living room. A couple of times, she tried to get Rose to eat something, but she didn't argue when Rose said no.

Rose washed Brody's face and stood on a chair to rinse out the baby food jar at the sink. She took Brody out of his seat and put him on the floor. He immediately crawled away, heading for a ball that had rolled against the fridge on the other side of the kitchen.

Mommy was just coming back from the living room again when Brody crawled into the doorway. She tripped over him and almost fell, grabbing a chair to steady herself. Brody started crying, but Rose didn't know if he was hurt or just scared.

"What are you doing?" Mommy yelled. "Why is he in the middle of the floor? Just get him out of here! Go put him to bed or something!"

Rose started crying too, even though she knew Mommy was worried about Daddy and that's why she was yelling. She didn't like Mommy yelling at her for any reason.

Mommy looked like she was going to yell again, but instead she took a couple of big breaths before she said anything. She picked up Brody and hugged him and rocked him until he stopped crying.

"I'm sorry," she said to Rose. "I shouldn't have yelled. It's going to be okay." She put one arm around Rose and hugged her too.

Rose didn't know if it really was going to be okay, but she hugged Mommy back. She loved Mommy, and she wanted her to be happy. She loved Daddy too, but that was more complicated.

"I can put Brody to bed," Rose said to Mommy. She wanted to do something to make things better. She also thought it would be better if Brody was already asleep when Daddy got home.

Mommy hesitated for a moment, then said, "Okay, Rose. That would be a big help. Thank you." She kissed Brody's forehead and handed him to Rose.

Brody squirmed and cried when Rose took him. Rose staggered a little with his weight, but she got her balance and carried him down the hall to his room.

Brody didn't want to go to bed. Rose changed his diaper and put his pajamas on, but when she tried

to put him in his crib, he cried. She sang to him, to try to get him to fall asleep, but he kept crying and sitting up. Finally, she climbed into his crib with him and lay down next to him. That worked a little, but he was still awake and squirmy, so she stroked his hair and sang to him for a while. After a while, he stopped moving around, and his breathing got slower and deeper.

Rose thought she should go back to her own room and do her homework, but she was afraid Brody would wake up when she climbed out of the crib. Instead, she lay there listening to Mommy walk back and forth in the living room. A few times, Daddy hadn't come home at night at all, and Rose hoped that would happen tonight. When he came home late, he was scary. Sometimes he was scary when he didn't come home late, too.

Rose thought she remembered a long time ago when Daddy hadn't been scary. Sometimes now he was nice, and he would tease her and tickle her and hug her. But she was never sure when he would stop being nice and start being scary. One minute he might be laughing and the next he would be shouting. Or worse.

The shouting woke Rose up. At first, she didn't know where she was, and then she realized she was still in Brody's crib. Brody was asleep, but he was making little noises and moving around, and Rose thought the shouting must be bothering him, too.

She heard a crash from down the hall and then more shouting. She climbed out of the crib, trying not to jiggle Brody. She was scared, but she was worried about Mommy. She opened the door, and the noise got louder. In the crib, Brody gave a little whimper, so she went out into the hall and shut the door.

She crept down the hall toward the living room and kitchen. She had started shaking now. The noise of Daddy shouting and Mommy crying got louder as she got closer. She stopped when she got to the end of the hall. She could see they weren't in the living room, and she was afraid to look around the corner into the kitchen.

There was another crash, and Rose jumped. Daddy was still shouting. He was yelling words, but Rose couldn't understand them. Once, Mommy yelled back, but then she stopped and just cried again.

Rose took a deep breath and tried to be brave, and then she looked around the corner. The first thing she saw was broken glass and broken dishes. The chicken and rice Mommy had made for supper was splattered on the floor and the cupboards. Daddy was standing with his back to Rose.

For a second, Rose didn't see Mommy, and then she saw her behind Daddy. Mommy was sitting on the floor against the wall, with her knees pulled up and her hands over her face. Then she took her hands down, and Rose saw that the side of

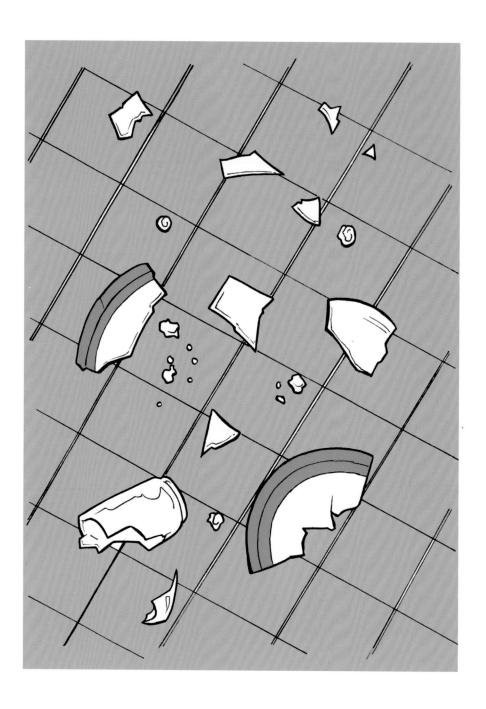

Mommy's face was red and puffy and blood was coming out of her nose.

Rose threw herself across the room toward Mommy. Daddy had hit her again! It was bad enough when Daddy yelled and said mean things, but Rose was terrified when he hit Mommy. When Daddy got angry, he wasn't Daddy anymore; he seemed to change into a thunderstorm or a wild bear—something dark and dangerous.

Mommy saw Rose just before Rose got to her and held out her arms. Rose fell into the hug and wrapped her arms around Mommy's neck. She could feel Mommy shaking and she didn't like that. Mommy being scared was awful.

For a long time, she kept her face buried in Mommy's shoulder, but then she realized Daddy had stopped yelling. She turned her head a little so she could look over to where Daddy had been standing.

He was still standing there, but he wasn't saying anything. He was breathing hard and staring at Mommy and Rose, opening and closing his hands like he didn't know what to do with them. When he saw Rose looking at him, he closed his eyes, and when he opened them again, Rose thought maybe he was crying too. But she couldn't tell for sure, because he turned around and walked out of the room. She heard the front door slam and then the sound of Daddy's car driving away. In the other room, Brody started to cry.

An hour later, Rose lay in her own bed, with Mommy next to her, holding her. Mommy had soothed Brody and gotten him to go back to sleep, and then she had gone to wash the blood off her face. The whole time, she kept saying to Rose, "It's okay. It will be okay. We'll be fine for the rest of the night."

Rose didn't know if Mommy was right or not, but she was still scared. She followed Mommy from

Brody's room to the bathroom, because she didn't want to let her out of her sight. Finally, Mommy agreed to sleep in Rose's bed.

"It's going to be okay, Rose," Mommy said again as she held her. "Go to sleep."

But it took Rose a very long time to fall asleep.

When Rose woke up the next morning, Mommy was gone, and Rose started worrying again. She got up and went into the kitchen. Mommy was there making coffee, and she'd cleaned up all the broken glass and spilled food. She turned around and smiled at Rose, and the sight of her face scared Rose all over again. The whole side of Mommy's face was swollen and purple, and her eye didn't open all the way.

"Mommy, are you okay?" Rose ran across the kitchen to bury her face in Mommy's stomach.

"I'm okay," Mommy said. "Sit down and eat some breakfast and then go get dressed for school."

"I can't go to school," Rose said.

"Why not?" Mommy asked.

"I just can't. I can't." Rose didn't want to leave Mommy and Brody alone. She was afraid of what might happen to them.

Maybe Mommy understood, because she didn't argue anymore.

For the rest of the morning, Rose sat on the couch with Mommy, cuddled into her side. They watched kid shows on TV, while Brody crawled around on the floor and played with toys. Mommy had left the curtains closed and the living room was dim. Rose thought it felt kind of like a dream. A few times, the phone rang, and Mommy would jump and then hug Rose tighter, but she didn't answer the phone.

They had been sitting on the couch for a long time—Rose thought a few hours, but she didn't know—when the doorbell rang. Mommy jumped again, and Rose felt her body go all tight and stiff.

They didn't move. Maybe the person would go away, Rose thought. But the doorbell rang again, and then someone knocked and rattled the door-knob.

Rose looked at Mommy, wondering if she should do something, but Mommy still didn't move.

The person knocked again, and then called through the door, "Monica! Open the door! I know you're in there!"

"I think it's Naomi," Rose whispered to Mommy. Naomi was Mommy's best friend.

Mommy didn't say anything, and Naomi called again, "Come on, Mon! I'm going to call the police if you don't open this door!"

The thought of the police made Rose's stomach jump. "I'm going to let her in," she said.

She slipped out from under Mommy's arm and stood up. Mommy leaned forward and put her hands over her face, but she didn't say anything as Rose ran over to the front door and opened it.

"Rose!" Naomi said, looking startled. "Why aren't you in school? What's going on?"

Rose didn't know what to say, so she grabbed Naomi's hand and pulled her into the house. "Please help Mommy," she said. "I don't know what to do."

Naomi hurried into the living room, looking worried. She turned the lights on and knelt down in front of Mommy and took her hands away from her face. "Oh sweetie," she said, and pulled Mommy into a hug. "This has to stop. You know that. It has to stop right now."

"But we don't know how to make Daddy stop," Rose said. "He gets mad even if we don't do anything."

"This is not your fault, darling." Naomi reached out to pull her into the hug. "It's not your Mommy's fault and it's not your fault and it's not Brody's fault."

"I don't know if I can do it," Mommy said.

"You can do it," Naomi said. "Do it for yourself. Do it for the kids. Do it for Trent, even. Do it because it's the right thing to do."

Rose didn't know what she was talking about. Trent was her Daddy, but what was it that Naomi was telling Mommy to do?

Mommy took a deep breath. She looked at Brody pushing a toy car back and forth across the floor, and then looked at Rose.

"You're right," she said to Naomi. "I just don't know if I can do it."

"I'll help you," Naomi said. "I will do anything you need me to do. How about I take Rose to pack a bag, while you get your own things together?"

Mommy didn't say anything for a few minutes, then she whispered, "Okay."

"Good," Naomi said. She pulled Mommy up from the couch and then took Rose's hand. "Come on, Rose. Do you have a suitcase?"

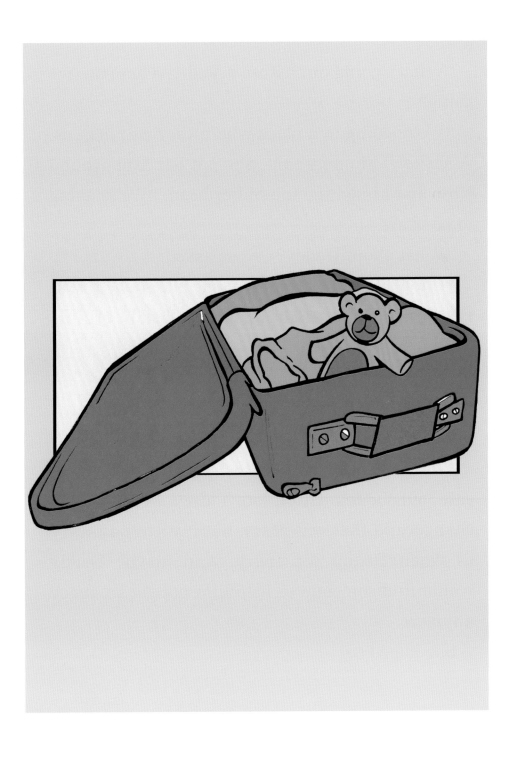

"What's going on?" Rose asked. "Where are we going?"

"We're going to a place where they can help us. A shelter," Mommy said. She put her arm around Rose and kissed the top of her head. "We're going to be okay."

"What about Daddy?" Rose asked.

"I don't know," Mommy said. She looked worried again. "That will be up to your Daddy, I think. He'll need to get help."

"I love him," Rose said. "But he's scary, too."

"I know," Mommy said. "I feel the same way." She picked up Brody.

Rose still felt confused as she packed her suitcase, but she felt better, too. Things were going to change, and that was scary, but it wasn't as scary as when Daddy got angry. And maybe Daddy would find someone to help him not get so angry anymore.

She hoped so.

Naming the Anger at Home

Many households experience uncontrollable anger at home. In the story you just read, Rose and her family are going through what is called domestic violence. Any physical abuse directed at a spouse, wife or husband, is considered domestic violence. It includes punching, shoving, or any other violent acts that one spouse commits against another. It's usually husbands that hurt their wives, though in rare cases, it's the other way around.

Often domestic violence also includes verbal abuse. This means that it includes not just physical acts, like hitting, but also abusive language—the kind of words that hurt people's feelings or make them feel bad about themselves. A husband might call his wife cruel names, for example, or a boyfriend could tell his girlfriend that she's worthless, and make her believe it.

Understand the Word

Domestic partners are people who have a long-term relationship and live in the same house. Married couples are one type of domestic partnership, but two people don't have to be married to be considered domestic partners.

Kids and Domestic Violence

Although domestic violence happens between **domestic partners**, it also affects lots of children. Many

Sometimes parents get upset and frustrated about things that are going on in their lives, but that still doesn't mean it's okay for them to hit someone or break things.

of the women who are abused have kids, and these children have to learn to live with the violence going on in their houses. It's estimated that almost 3.5 million children have to deal with domestic violence at home, every year. That's a lot of kids who live with fear and anger at home, and Rose's predicament is unfortunately all too common.

Why Does Daddy Hit Mommy?

There are lots of reasons that domestic violence happens. Most of them have to do with issues of power and control. If one partner in a relationship feels the need to control the other, or to control the world around him, then sometimes that need takes the form of abuse and violence. A lot of the time, it's fathers that feel this need to control. Our culture tells men that they have to take care of their families, and to provide food and shelter. Often, losing a job or being poor makes dads feel like they aren't able to do that. They feel like they aren't in control of their families. Maybe they can't find another job, and they feel frustrated and scared and angry. Instead of doing something **constructive**, they take control of their families and their lives with violence.

Our culture also allows more violent behavior in men than women. Think about all the action movies you've seen. Most of the heroes are men with weapons and lots of muscle power. Soldiers are usually thought of as men, and little boys are encouraged to play with toy guns and violent video games. Little girls, on the other hand, are supposed to play house with dolls or have tea parties. There are also fewer images of women being violent on TV or in movies. All this adds up to the message that it's more okay for men to be violent than women. Some men take this to mean that they can be violent toward their families.

Sometimes drugs and alcohol help cause domestic violence. Fathers and mothers who are addicted to alcohol or drugs aren't in control of their behavior all the time. While they might be perfectly good parents when they're not under the influence of drugs, when they are, they can be angry, out-of-control, and violent. A person that is addicted to drugs or alcohol

Understand the Word

Something that is helpful is **constructive**. Criticism can be constructive if it helps people improve themselves, though it is not constructive if it puts them down and insults them.

might also be frustrated that they can't stay **sober,** and take that frustration out on their family.

Child Abuse and Domestic Violence

If parents direct violence toward their children, it's called child abuse. Sometimes a parent that commits domestic violence also commits child abuse, but they aren't necessarily the same thing. However, kids who witness domestic violence aren't safe from its effects. Seeing one parent hit another can be very **traumatic**. It makes home a scary place.

Being Angry

Kids who live in homes with domestic violence react differently to the anger and hurt they witness. Some kids, like Rose, get scared for the parent that's the victim of abuse. Rose was worried for her mother, and tried to protect her when she saw her dad hitting her. Another kid might react to the same situation with anger. If he saw his dad hitting his mom,

Understand the Word

A person that is not under the influence of a drug or alcohol is **sober**. The opposite of sober is intoxicated.

An experience is **traumatic** if it shocks or hurts you in some way. Something can be physically traumatic, if it causes physical hurt, or emotionally traumatic, if it makes you feel upset and shocked.

he might yell at his dad, but a lot of kids also get mad at their friends or siblings, just to release some of the stress and anger they feel at home.

If you've experienced domestic violence, it's okay to be scared or angry. Those feelings are natural responses to a very difficult situation, and you shouldn't try to bottle up your emotions. On the other hand, you want to make sure you're in control of your emotions.

When you live around domestic violence, you might feel scared or angry or like you have no one to turn to. Those are normal feelings, but you aren't really alone and there are people who can help.

You don't want to get so angry with a friend that you hurt his feelings or punch him. If you did that, you'd be continuing the violence that made you so upset in the first place. You also shouldn't be sad or scared all the time. If you feel that way, look for someone to talk to about it.

When Abuse Seems "Normal"

If you have to worry about domestic violence all the time, it's hard to live a normal life. What's "normal" in your house isn't the same normal that other kids experience. Like Rose, you might be scared at home all the time, even though your house should be somewhere you feel safe and comfortable. You probably can't invite friends over to your house if your dad is yelling all the time, or if your mom has a black eye.

You might also have to grow up faster than other kids. Rose had to feed her baby brother, change his diaper, and put him to bed. She seems pretty grown up, and doesn't even complain about having to do any of this. Lots of kids who experience domestic violence have to take a lot more responsibility at home than their friends do. Sometimes they have to take care of younger siblings, cook, and clean. It's hard to be a normal kid when everything at your house is turned upside down.

Kids and Domestic Violence

There are lots of other ways that domestic violence can change kids' lives. Here's a list of a few of them:

Understand the Word

Self-esteem is a feeling of pride in yourself. It means that you're happy with who you are. You like yourself.

• Kids who live with domestic violence are more likely to do poorly in school, since they have so much other stuff to worry about. However, they might also do really well in school, if they use schoolwork to take their minds off what's going on at home.

• Violence becomes more normal to kids who live with domestic violence, and they might start acting more violent toward other kids.

• Low **self-esteem** becomes an issue for kids who live with domestic violence, since they feel like it's their fault that all that violence is happening at home.

• Kids who live with domestic violence often become afraid of close relationships with anyone. After all, daddy and mommy are married, but it didn't stop them from having fights.

• Kids who live with domestic violence get sick more often, because they aren't eating right, can't get enough sleep, or are stressed out and worried all the time.

• Kids who live with domestic violence are likely to have more nightmares.

Even though kids may not be the ones who get bruises or broken bones from getting hit, domestic violence is hard on them!

Long-Term Impacts

Domestic violence also shapes kids' lives, even long after they've moved out of their houses or the violence has stopped. Kids who grow up in homes with domestic violence are much more likely to be arrested when they get older, to abuse alcohol and drugs, and to commit crimes against other people. Not all kids who grow up around domestic violence end up this way, but growing up in a violent and scary atmosphere leaves some pretty big scars. If your dad hits your mom, that doesn't mean you have to end up in jail—but it does mean you probably need some help coping with what's going on.

Getting Help Is Hard

Even though living at home with one parent that hits another one is really scary, asking for help can be even scarier. You don't know who to turn to, what to tell, or whether it will do any good. It took Rose's mom a long time to get up enough nerve to leave her dad, even though he was hurting her. It's also hard to leave one parent behind. Even if your dad hits your mom, he's still your dad, and you probably still love him. It's hard to move out of your house, knowing that you're not moving as a family.

How to Get Help

Getting help is really hard, but you have to do it at some point. Fortunately, because domestic violence is so common, there are a lot of people out there who want to help both parents and children. If you think that you've seen domestic abuse at home, then you should tell someone who can help you. A good place to start is at school. You can tell a teacher, a coach, or your school counselor. Counselors are adults who

It can be very hard for grownups to ask for help, too, even when they know that's what they need to do.

are trained to deal with students' problems, including domestic violence. They know how to deal with what you're experiencing, and they will listen to your story and get you some help.

A lot of towns and cities also have hotlines that are dedicated to helping people who are living with domestic violence, including children. Search around on the Internet or in your local phone book for telephone numbers you can call to tell someone about what's going on in your house. The National Domestic Violence Hotline at 800-799-SAFE is a country-wide number to call. There are concerned and knowledgeable people on the other end that can give you a lot of help and keep your problem **confidential**. You can call yourself, or urge your mom, dad, or older sibling to call instead.

In the story, Rose's mom was planning on going to a **shelter,** which is another source of help. There are many shelters for victims of domestic violence, which offer a safe place out of the house. It might be scary to move into a new place—but probably not as scary as staying at home.

Understand the Word

If you do something in secret, you are being **confidential**. **Shelters** are confidential because they don't tell anyone who is living there, or how to get in contact with them.

What Is a Shelter Like?

All shelters are different, but they have a few things in common. Living in a shelter is usually free. If you move to a shelter, you and your mom (or dad) and siblings probably have more important things to worry about than finding enough money to live, day by day. Shelters provide a roof over your head, a bed to sleep in, and food to fill your stomach. They also generally have a place to do your laundry, some parking spaces, and a little bit of storage for your stuff.

Understand the Word

Communal means that something belongs to many different people. Communal property is shared by several people, rather than owned by individuals who use it only for themselves.

You'll be living with lots of other people, which can be hard, but can also be a good experience. Shelters are **communal** living centers, where lots of people live together. You have to get along with other families that are sharing the same space, which can be a big adjustment if you're used to living in a single-family home. However, living with other families that have gone through domestic violence is also really helpful. You'll realize that there are other kids just like you, who have had to live with their parents' fights and being scared at home.

If you end up going to a shelter, the rooms will probably be very different than your bedroom at home. Everything might feel strange to you at first, but you and your family are safe there, and people are available to help you out.

Shelters also provide a lot more than just the basic necessities. They give you and your family emotional support, and help you decide on your next step. Shelters aren't supposed to be a permanent place to live; they are temporary living quarters for families that need to get away from violence. People at the shelter will help you find a new house, give your parent support in how to be a good parent for you, and will assist in any legal actions your parent might take. There will also be people for kids to talk to, who can help you get past all that hurt and anger you went through.

Getting Help for the Abuser

Even if a family finds a way to get away from domestic violence, the problem isn't truly solved until the abuser also gets help. If you and your mom leave home to stop your dad from committing domestic violence, you've taken a huge, important step, but your dad needs help too. It's harder to figure out how to help the parent you left behind, because he or she might not even want to be helped.

Sometimes an abuser realizes the damage that he or she has done once the rest of the family leaves the house. You can imagine what the end of Rose's story is once she and her mom and brother enter the shelter. Maybe her dad realizes that he's losing his family, and vows to be a better husband and father. He gets help with dealing with his anger, and eventually, he learns to control his temper and stop lashing out with violence.

Of course, it doesn't always work out this way. A lot of the time, abusers have serious problems that need professional help. If Rose's dad is addicted to alcohol,

You can't control what happens to your family. Things are never going to be perfect in any family, but you can find people to help you get through the hard times.

for example, he might need to enter a rehabilitation program where he fights his addiction before he can be reunited with his family. Or maybe his anger problems just run too deep, and he will have to get anger-management counseling if he hopes to see his kids again.

Hope

No kid should live in fear of entering her house, nor should anyone have to worry about his dad hurting his mom, or his mom hurting his dad. You have the right to feel safe—and remember, domestic violence is never your fault! You didn't do anything to cause any of the anger and hurt going on in your house.

There are lots of ways to get help for yourself, or for a friend you think might be witnessing domestic violence. As long as you find the strength to look for help, there are lots of people who are willing to give it. Even if you're in the worst situation imaginable, there's always hope!

Questions to Think About

1. How do you think that Rose's dad felt when his family left?

2. What can you imagine happening once Rose and her family got to the shelter?

3. Who else could have helped Rose, if Naomi hadn't visited?

4. What were some of the emotions that Rose felt during the whole story?

Further Reading

Bentrim, William George. *Mommy's Black Eye: Children Dealing with Domestic Violence.* Scotts Valley, Calif.: CreateSpace, 2009.

Carmichael, Katrina. *Daddy, Why Do You Hurt Mommy?* Detroit, Mich.: G Publishing, 2006.

Cefrey, Holly. *Domestic Violence.* New York: Rosen Publishing, 2008.

Davis, Diane. *Something is Wrong at My House: A Book About Parents' Fighting, Rev. ed.* Seattle, Wash.: Parenting Press, 2010.

Stark, Evan. *Everything You Need to Know About Family Violence.* New York: Rosen Publishing, 2001.

Find Out More on the Internet

Boys Town: Saving Children, Healing Families
www.boystown.org

Childhelp
www.childhelpusa.org

Domestic Abuse Project
www.domesticabuseproject.org

Domestic Violence Awareness Handbook
www.dm.usda.gov/shmd/aware.htm

National Domestic Violence Hotline
www.ndvh.org

The websites listed on this page were active at the time of publication. The publisher is not responsible for websites that have changed their address or discontinued operation since the date of publication. The publisher will review and update the websites upon each reprint.

Index

Picture Credits

Hofmeester, Patricia; fotolia: p. 40
Mackenzie, Jenn; fotolia: p. 28
Monkey Business; fotolia: p. 42
MyShotz.com; fotolia: p. 37
Petrowski, Margot; fotolia: p. 32

To the best knowledge of the publisher, all images not specifically credited are in the public domain. If any image has been inadvertently uncredited, please notify Harding House Publishing Service, 220 Front Street, Vestal, New York 13850, so that credit can be given in future printings.

About the Authors

Sheila Stewart has written several dozen books for young people, both fiction and nonfiction, although she especially enjoys writing fiction. She has a master's degree in English and now works as a writer and editor. She lives with her two children in a house overflowing with books, in the Southern Tier of New York State.

Rae Simons is a freelance author who has written numerous educational books for children and young adults. She also has degrees in psychology and special education, and she has worked with children encountering a range of troubles in their lives.

About the Consultant

Cindy Croft, M.A. Ed., is Director of the Center for Inclusive Child Care, a state-funded program with support from the McKnight Foundation, that creates, promotes, and supports pathways to successful inclusive care for all children. Its goal is inclusion and retention of children with disabilities and behavioral challenges in community child care settings. Cindy Croft is also on the faculty at Concordia University, where she teaches courses on young children with special needs and the emotional growth of young children. She is the author of several books, including *The Six Keys: Strategies for Promoting Children's Mental Health*.